13 Mistakes That Christians Make

We Are Not Holier Than Thou

Travis Peagler

Script Novel Publishing

CONTENTS

PREFACE

In "13 Mistakes That Christians Make: We Are Not Holier Than Thou", author Travis Peagler fearlessly exposes the common pitfalls that many Christians unknowingly and knowingly fall into, thereby hindering their spiritual growth and relationship with God. With a fresh perspective and insightful wisdom, this book shines a light on the flawed thinking and behaviors that often plague believers, ultimately leading them astray from their true purpose and calling.

From judgmental attitudes to legalistic mindsets, from prideful behaviors to misplaced priorities, this eye-opening guide delves into the 13 most critical mistakes that can sabotage a Christian's faith journey. Through real-life stories, practical advice, and scriptural truths, readers are encouraged to reflect, repent, and refocus on the grace and love of God.

Whether you're a seasoned believer or a newcomer to the faith, "13 Mistakes That Christians Make" serves as a wake-up call for those seeking to deepen their faith, inviting them to shed the facade of holier-than-thou attitudes and instead embrace humility, authenticity, and a genuine pursuit of God's heart. This book is a must-read for anyone striving to overcome the barriers that separate them from experiencing the fullness of God's blessings and presence in their lives.

Chapter One

THE MISTAKE OF LEGALISM: UNDERSTANDING THE TRUE ESSENCE OF CHRISTIANITY

The Pharisees were a Jewish sect during Jesus's time known for their strict adherence to the laws and traditions of their religion. They were seen as very focused on external practices such as rituals, tithing, and dietary restrictions while neglecting the deeper matters of the heart, such as love, mercy, and compassion.

In the New Testament, Jesus often clashed with the Pharisees, criticizing them for their legalism and hypocrisy. He condemned their focus on outward appearances and neglect of justice, mercy, and faithfulness.

In (Matthew 23:23), Jesus rebukes the Pharisees, saying, "Woe to you, teachers of the law and Pharisees, you hypocrites! You give a tenth of your spices—mint, dill, and cumin. But you have neglected the more important matters of the law—justice, mercy, and faithfulness. You should have practiced the latter without neglecting the former."

Regrettably, the Pharisees' ideologies did not perish with them. Even today, we encounter individuals within the church who mirror their pharisaical tendencies. These are people who, despite their zeal for religious practices and rules, lack love and compassion for others. They are swift to judge and condemn, neglecting the grace and forgiveness that Jesus's message embodies.

It is important for us as believers to examine our own hearts and motivations and to strive to embody the love and compassion that Jesus taught. We should seek to follow his example of reaching out to the marginalized, showing mercy to the hurting, and standing up for justice for the oppressed. This is the true essence of Christianity, and it is what sets us apart from the legalistic and hypocritical attitudes of the Pharisees.

Legalism is a trap that many Christians fall into, either unintentionally or intentionally. The mistake of legalism lies in putting too much emphasis on following rules and regulations rather than focusing on the heart and the relationship with God. Some Christians may fall into legalism unintentionally due to a lack of understanding of grace and the freedom we have in Christ. They may believe that by strictly adhering to a set of rules and regulations, they can earn God's favor and salvation. However, this is not true; man could not keep God's laws in the days of Moses, and we surely can't keep them now. It simply proved to be too difficult for us to do so, for we've all fallen short of the Glory of God (Romans 3:23). This legalistic mindset can lead to feelings of guilt, shame, and judgment towards themselves and others who do not live up to their standards.

On the other hand, some Christians may intentionally embrace legalism as a means of control or self-righteousness. They may use rules and regulations to manipulate others, assert their authority, or feel superior to those who do not follow the same strict standards. This kind of legalism can be harmful to relationships within the church and your family and hinder the true message of grace and love that Christ preached.

The mistake of legalism is contrary to the teachings of Jesus, who emphasized the importance of love, mercy, and compassion over rigid adherence to the law. Christians should be mindful of avoiding legalism and instead strive to live out their faith in a spirit of grace and humility, recognizing that salvation comes through faith in Christ, not through works or rule-following. It's important to note that God freed us from the law through Christ, but if you follow the old laws, you'll be judged according to those laws, stripping you of grace through Jesus Christ.

To put it plainly, you're doomed because no one can keep the laws as mentioned before. For those who choose to keep these laws, it is like a person being set free from prison, and they turn and walk back into the cell in which they were freed, shut the cell door, and toss out the key. Does this make sense? I guess if one has been enslaved by rejecting Jesus, it may make perfect sense. Christ said He is Lord of the Sabbath (Matthew 12:8) and has also fulfilled the law. What does this mean? It means that the chapter is complete and that we're now living in the chapter called 'Grace'. Jesus took us out of the law and placed us under grace. (John 1:17) highlights: "For the Law was given through Moses; grace and truth were realized through Jesus Christ."

Consider this parable below:

The sun was starting to set, casting a warm orange glow over the sleepy town of Bethel. People went about their daily routines, each one carrying the weight of their own worries and sins. Among them was a young man named Daniel, a devout follower of the Christian faith. He attended the local church, listened to the sermons faithfully, and obeyed every rule and regulation set by the religious leaders.

But deep within his heart, Daniel wrestled with a profound sense of unease. Despite his unwavering devotion, he couldn't shake the nagging feeling that Christianity had become nothing but a set of rigid rules and legalistic practices. It seemed as though the true essence of his faith had been lost amidst all the regulations and expectations, a sentiment that many of us may resonate with.

One evening, Daniel gathered the courage to discuss his concerns with his close friend and mentor, Pastor John. They sat on a bench outside the church, a gentle breeze playing with their hair as Daniel poured out his troubled thoughts.

"Pastor John, I have devoted my life to practicing Christianity to the best of my ability, but it feels like I'm missing something. I feel suffocated by all these rules and regulations, and it's hindering my relationship with God. I can't help but wonder if there's more to Christianity than legalism."

Pastor John, with his eyes filled with compassion, listened intently. He understood the struggle Daniel was facing; he had seen it in numerous others who came seeking solace and clarity. His presence and understanding offered a glimmer of hope in the midst of Daniel's confusion.

"My dear Daniel, you are not alone in these thoughts. Legalism has become a trap for many believers, distorting the true essence of Christianity. It is essential to understand that our faith is not about following a set of rules or earning salvation through our own efforts. It is about a deep and personal relationship with our Creator, who loved us so much that He sent His Son to die for our sins."

Daniel leaned in, eager to hear more. His heart longed for a true understanding of what it meant to be a Christian beyond the constraints of legalism.

Pastor John continued, "Legalism often leads to pride and judgment, as people believe they are more righteous than others because they follow stricter rules or maintain a certain lifestyle. However, true Christianity is rooted in grace and love, as Jesus taught us. It is about surrendering our lives to Him and allowing His transforming power to work within us."

Daniel nodded, a spark of hope and excitement filling his eyes. He realized that the mistake of legalism had been holding him back from experiencing the fullness of his faith. He suddenly felt a newfound freedom, knowing that he didn't have to strive to earn God's love but rather embrace it with humility and gratitude.

As the sun set behind the horizon, Daniel and Pastor John continued their conversation, diving deeper into the true essence of Christianity. This was just the beginning of Daniel's journey towards a more authentic and fulfilling faith, one that would reshape his understanding of God's immense love and grace.

Little did Daniel know, this realization would not only transform his own life but also inspire others in the community to reevaluate their understanding of Christianity and rediscover the essence that had been overshadowed by legalism.

End of Parable

Know or recall that the Holy Spirit teaches us, and never ignore the convictions you feel in your heart, as it may be the Holy Spirit knocking at the door.

The Lord's greatest commandment is love; please remember this. Love God with all your mind, heart, and soul (Matthew 22:37).

CHAPTER TWO

THE MISTAKE OF HYPOCRISY: LIVING A GENUINE FAITH

In today's world, it is not uncommon to see individuals who claim to live a life of faith but fail to exhibit genuine actions that align with their beliefs. This discrepancy between what one says and how they actually live is known as hypocrisy. It is a mistake that can have significant consequences not only for the individual but also for their relationships and the impact they have on those around them.

Hypocrisy in the context of faith occurs when someone proclaims to believe in certain values, principles, or religious teachings, but their actions do not reflect these beliefs. It is a contradiction that undermines the credibility of one's faith and casts doubt upon the authenticity of one's professed commitment. As Jesus Himself condemned the religious leaders of His time, "Woe to you, teachers of the law and Pharisees, you hypocrites! You clean the outside of the cup and dish, but inside they are full of greed and self-indulgence" (Matthew 23:25).

Living a genuine faith-filled life requires consistent alignment between one's beliefs and actions. It necessitates a sincere devotion to one's spiritual journey, personally and in relation to others. One cannot simply claim faith without actively living it out in one's daily life. As James, the brother of Jesus, poignantly stated, "But be doers of the word, and not hearers only, deceiving yourselves" (James 1:22). We're all fallible, yes we are, but the difference is this, do we enjoy swimming in sin, are we desperately trying to escape the sin pool, or do we occasionally fall in?

Do you repent with a sincere heart before God? Repentance is not a Christian's get-out-of-jail-free card. We can't trick God, even though many of us try; God knows who's sincere and who is not. (Hebrews 10:26-27) warns: "For if we go on sinning deliberately after receiving the knowledge of the truth, no sacrifice for sins is left, but only a fearful expectation of judgment and of raging fire that will consume the enemies of God." Paul also writes in (Romans 6:15-16): "What then? Shall we sin because we are not under the law but under grace? By no means! Don't you know that when you offer yourselves to someone as obedient slaves, you are slaves of the one you obey—whether you are slaves to sin, which leads to death, or to obedience, which leads to righteousness?"

The mistake of hypocrisy is dangerous because it deceives not only others but also the individual. It breeds a sense of complacency and self-righteousness, leading one to believe they are fulfilling their religious obligations while neglecting the true essence of faith. The danger lies in hypocrisy blinding individuals to their own faults and preventing them from recognizing the need for personal growth and transformation.

Living a genuine faith-filled life requires self-reflection, humility, and an ongoing commitment to spiritual growth. It involves acknowledging and addressing one's weaknesses and shortcomings, seeking forgiveness and reconciliation when necessary, and continually striving to align one's actions with their professed beliefs. It requires a willingness to admit mistakes, learn from them, and make amends rather than concealing or denying them. It's okay to admit when you're wrong; everyone wants to be right, but God is the only one that's right, so let's abide by His word.

Ultimately, a genuine faith-filled life is characterized by love, compassion, and a genuine desire to serve others. It is not about putting on a show or seeking external validation but about seeking to emulate the example set by Jesus Christ. It is about being honest with oneself and others, acknowledging one's imperfections, and committing to a lifelong journey of personal and spiritual growth.

In conclusion, the mistake of hypocrisy in living a genuine faith-filled life can have significant consequences. It undermines the authenticity of one's beliefs and damages relationships and the ability to make a positive impact in the world. Living a genuine faith-filled life requires consistent alignment between one's beliefs and actions, self-reflection, humility, and ongoing commitment to personal growth. By avoiding the mistake of hypocrisy and striving to live a genuine faith-filled life, one can experience true fulfillment and make a positive difference in the lives of others.

Chapter Three

THE MISTAKE OF JUDGMENT: EMBRACING ACCEPTANCE AND FORGIVENESS

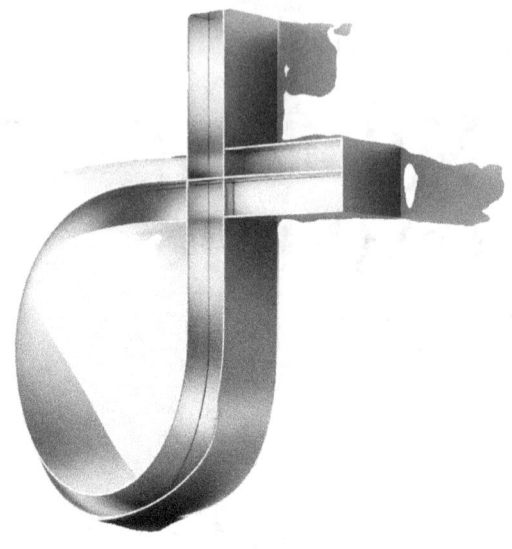

In the Bible, the concept of judgment is often viewed in both a positive and negative light. One mistake of judgment frequently warned against in the Bible is the act of passing judgment on others in a harsh or hypocritical manner. In (Matthew 7:1-5), Jesus says, "Do not judge, or you too will be judged. For in the same way you judge others, you will be judged, and with the measure you use, it will be measured to you." This warns against making unfair or harsh judgments of others, as we will be held to the same standard ourselves.

Another mistake of judgment mentioned in the Bible is the act of relying solely on human wisdom and understanding rather than seeking God's guidance and wisdom. (Proverbs 3:5-6) instructs us to "Trust in the Lord with all your heart and lean not on your own understanding; in all your ways submit to him, and he will make your paths straight." Relying on our own judgment without seeking God's guidance can lead to mistakes and missteps.

Recall, too, that in the Bible, the concept of making a mistake in judgment is often referred to as "falling into sin" or "erring in judgment." One notable example is seen in the story of David and Bathsheba (2 Samuel 11:1-27). David's decision to commit adultery with Bathsheba and then conspire to have her husband Uriah killed because she became pregnant was a grave mistake in judgment that resulted in severe consequences.

Additionally, the Bible warns against judging others harshly or unjustly, as seen in (Matthew 7:1-5) where Jesus teaches, "Do not judge, or you too will be judged. For in the same way you judge others, you will be judged, and with the measure you use, it will be measured to you."

The Bible teaches that we should be cautious in our judgments of others, seek wisdom and guidance from God, and strive to act with fairness, humility, and compassion in all our interactions.

When it comes to forgiveness, let me start by stating that everything in this universe is forgivable except one single thing, and that's blasphemy against the Holy Spirit. Blasphemy against the Holy Spirit will not be forgiven in this world or the next (Matthew 12:31-32). Imagine that there is only one thing that God will not forgive us for.

In our journey through life, we often find ourselves facing moments of regret and making mistakes. These mistakes can range from minor errors in judgment to major missteps that have a significant impact on our lives and the lives of others. However, one of the biggest mistakes we can make is refusing to accept and forgive ourselves for these errors.

Acceptance is a crucial step towards healing and growth. It allows us to acknowledge our mistakes without judgment or shame. When we accept that we have made a mistake, we can begin to understand the underlying factors that led to our actions. This self-reflection helps us learn from our mistakes and make better choices in the future.

Forgiveness is another essential aspect of moving forward. It involves letting go of resentment and anger towards ourselves. When we hold onto these negative emotions, they can eat away at us and prevent us from experiencing true happiness and peace. By forgiving ourselves, we free ourselves from the burden of our mistakes and open ourselves up to new possibilities.

Embracing acceptance and forgiveness is not an easy task. It requires humility and a willingness to confront our flaws and weaknesses. We must be willing to look within ourselves honestly and without judgment. It also takes time and effort to cultivate a mindset of acceptance and forgiveness. However, the rewards are immeasurable.

When we learn to accept and forgive ourselves, we become more compassionate and understanding towards others. We recognize that everyone is fallible and prone to making mistakes. This understanding allows us to extend forgiveness to

others, creating a cycle of healing and growth in our relationships.

Moreover, accepting and forgiving ourselves allows us to
learn from our mistakes and continue to move forward. It
gives us the courage to take risks and make changes in our
lives, knowing that if we stumble, we can pick ourselves up
and try again.

Many of us fall prey to the mistake of judgment. However, by
embracing acceptance and forgiveness, we can heal and grow
from our mistakes. It is through these acts of self-compassion
and understanding that we can create a more fulfilling and
meaningful life for ourselves and those around us. Let us
have the strength to embrace acceptance and forgiveness and
experience their transformative power.

It's also important to forgive others who have wronged or
sinned against us. Consider (Matthew 6:14-15) - "For if you
forgive other people when they sin against you, your heavenly
Father will also forgive you. But if you do not forgive others,
your Father will not forgive your sins." Ironically, you'll find
folks who want God to forgive them for their misdeeds but

still have ill feelings and unforgiveness for those who hurt them, and in return, they have not forgiven them.

So, if you find that you're struggling to forgive, check your heart, as I can assure you that Satan is accusing you.   In (Revelation 12:10), Satan is described as the one who accuses believers before God, day and night. This aspect of Satan's character is seen as deceitful and malicious, as he seeks to lead people astray and bring false accusations against them.

Ultimately, the belief is that through faith in Jesus Christ, believers can overcome Satan's accusations and temptations, as God's grace and forgiveness prevail over the accuser's lies. So, I hope that you rest in that peace.

CHAPTER FOUR

THE MISTAKE OF NEGLECTING SPIRITUAL GROWTH

S ome people fail to realize that accepting Christ as Lord and Savior is just the beginning of their journey, not the end. God never intended us to live our entire lives as a baby or a toddler. Life is all about growth and spiritual growth once we accept Jesus Christ as Lord.

After accepting Christ as Lord and Savior, it is important for believers to continue to grow and deepen their faith. This includes studying the Bible regularly, praying consistently, participating in fellowship with other believers, and serving others with love and compassion.

God desires for us to mature in our faith, becoming more like Jesus in our thoughts, actions, and attitudes. This process of spiritual growth, often referred to as sanctification, involves surrendering to the work of the Holy Spirit in our lives and allowing God to transform us from the inside out.

As we grow in our faith, we experience an increasing sense of intimacy with God and a greater understanding of His purposes for our lives. We develop spiritual maturity, gaining wisdom and discernment to navigate the challenges and complexities of life.

Living as a mature believer means fully embracing the call to love and serve others, to share the message of salvation with those who do not know Christ, and to live a life that reflects the character of God. It is a journey of ongoing transformation, as we continually seek to align our hearts and minds with the will of God.

Ultimately, the goal of the Christian life is to become more like Christ, growing in holiness and becoming a beacon of light and hope in a world that is in desperate need of God's love and truth. Let us embrace the journey of faith with humility, courage, and perseverance, trusting in God's grace to lead us toward a deeper and richer relationship with Him.

In today's fast-paced and busy world, it is easy to get caught up in the hustle and bustle of everyday life. We often prioritize our jobs, relationships, and personal goals, neglecting an essential aspect of our lives – our spiritual growth. Cultivating a deeper relationship with God is crucial for our overall well-being and fulfillment.

Many of us may have grown up with some religious or spiritual practices, attending church services or participating in rituals. However, as we get older and face various challenges and responsibilities, we may find ourselves slowly drifting away from these practices.

Neglecting our spiritual growth can have significant consequences. Without a strong connection with God, we may feel lost, anxious, and unfulfilled. When we do not make an effort to deepen our relationship with a higher power, we miss out on the peace, guidance, and strength that spiritual practices provide. It is like trying to navigate through life without a compass – we may find ourselves constantly searching for direction and purpose.

So, how can we cultivate a deeper relationship with God?

Firstly, it is important to set aside time each day for spiritual practices. This may include prayer, meditation, reading the Bible, or engaging in acts of service. Giving ourselves space to connect with God allows us to quiet our minds, reflect on our blessings, and seek guidance for our lives. Whether it is a few minutes in the morning or a longer period later in the day, making this time a priority is essential.

Secondly, finding a community of like-minded individuals can be incredibly beneficial. Joining a religious group, attending worship services, or participating in study groups provides a support system and a space for growth. Sharing our spiritual journeys with others allows us to learn from their experiences and encourages us to stay committed to our own spiritual path.

Additionally, we must be open to spiritual growth and willing to learn and evolve. This may involve questioning our beliefs, exploring new perspectives, and challenging ourselves to go beyond our comfort zones. Embracing growth requires humility and a willingness to let go of preconceived notions or dogmas that may limit our understanding of God.

Lastly, integrating our spiritual practices into our everyday lives is crucial. Rather than treating spirituality as something separate from our day-to-day activities, we can infuse it into our work, relationships, and decision-making processes. By doing so, we align our actions with our beliefs and create a more harmonious and purposeful existence.

Cultivating a deeper relationship with God is not a one-time event but a lifelong journey. It requires consistent effort and a genuine desire to connect with a higher power. By prioritizing our spiritual growth, we can experience profound peace, love, and fulfillment, enriching not just our own lives, but the lives of those around us. Let us not make the mistake of neglecting our spiritual well-being, for it is in this relationship with God that we truly find ourselves and our purpose.

Chapter Five

The Mistake of Fear: Trusting in God's Sovereignty

F ear and trust are powerful emotions that can significantly impact our physical relationships. When we are afraid, we may hold back from fully engaging in a physical relationship, fearing vulnerability or rejection. This fear can manifest in various ways, such as avoiding physical intimacy, being hesitant to open up emotionally, or even creating distance between us and our partner.

Let me be clear: God has not given us the spirit of fear, so whenever that spirit knocks at your door, you know who sent it. In Jesus' name, I pray that you 'return to sender,' the father of lies. It amazes me how some Christians act like Satan is not prowling suburban neighborhoods, inner city streets, and country roads. We can't pretend the threat is not real; know thy enemy. Satan aims to undermine people's faith in God and His word. By instilling trepidation, the Devil seeks to separate individuals from their belief in God's love, truth, promises, and protection. He tries to pull you away from God to have his way with you.

The Devil seeks to gain control over people's hearts and minds by causing fear and doubt. He thrives on chaos, confusion, and the breakdown of faith, which strengthens his hold over individuals. By sowing seeds of distrust and deception, the

Devil seeks to manipulate and deceive people, leading them away from God's plan for their lives.

In our journey of understanding and living in the truth of God's sovereignty, it is important to recognize the mistake of allowing fear to hinder our trust in Him. Fear has a way of paralyzing us, making us doubt the very nature and goodness of God. When we let fear dictate our actions and decisions, we are essentially saying that we do not believe in God's ability to handle the situations we face.

Fear is a natural response to uncertainty and the unknown. It is a human instinct that keeps us safe and helps us survive dangerous situations. However, when fear becomes our primary focus, and we start to see everything through its lens, we lose sight of how big God is and become consumed by our own limited perspective.

Trusting in God's sovereignty means acknowledging that He controls all things, including the things we fear. It means realizing that no matter what may come our way, God can work everything out for our good and His glory.

In the Bible, we are repeatedly reminded not to be afraid. (Isaiah 41:10) says, "So do not fear, for I am with you; do not be dismayed, for I am your God. I will strengthen you and help you; I will uphold you with my righteous right hand." This verse assures us that God is not only present with us in our fear but also actively working on our behalf.

Trusting in God's plan requires us to relinquish control and surrender our fears to Him. It means releasing our grip on our own plans and desires and submitting them to His will. It means choosing to believe in His goodness, even when circumstances suggest otherwise.

When we allow fear to overtake our trust in God's sovereignty, we are essentially limiting His power and preventing Him from working in and through us. We become bound by fear, unable to step out in faith and obedience.

However, when we choose to trust in God's governance despite our fear, we open ourselves up to the incredible blessings and opportunities that He has in store for us. We are able to walk in the peace and confidence that comes from knowing that God is in control.

Trusting in God's goodness does not mean that we will never face difficulties or that everything will always go according to our own plans. It means we have faith that God is working all things together for our ultimate good and His glory, re-gardless of our present circumstances. For all things work for good for those that love the Lord.

So, let us not make the mistake of allowing fear to hinder our trust in God's protection. Instead, let us place our burdens and fears in His capable hands and walk in the peace and freedom that comes from truly trusting in Him. Please know that God allows us to go through trials and tribulations to help us grow, test, and build our faith and long-suffering so that peace can have her perfect work in us because God loves us.

Chapter Six

The Mistake of Division

I've always been fascinated by how we came to have many different denominations from one Bible. Are there really that many ways to interpret God's word, or is it man? I know the existence of multiple denominations with different interpretations of the Bible can be a complex and sensitive topic for many people. I believe diversity of interpretations comes from a variety of factors, including differences in cultural backgrounds, theological perspectives, historical contexts, personal experiences, and even Satan.

It's important to remember that the Bible is a complex and ancient text that has been translated and interpreted by many people over centuries. Different denominations may place different emphasis on certain passages, teachings, or traditions, leading to distinctive interpretations of the same text.

Additionally, human nature and individual biases can also play a role in shaping interpretations of religious texts. We all have our own perspectives, beliefs, and cultural influences that can color how we understand and apply the teachings of the Bible. Essentially, pastors need to maintain a balance between delivering their message effectively and avoiding the temptation to seek validation through applause or performance. The primary responsibility of a pastor is to faithfully preach and teach the word of God, guiding their congregation towards spiritual growth and understanding.

Being mindful of the intention behind their actions and ensuring that their focus remains on serving and leading the flock can help pastors avoid getting caught up in the spotlight or seeking personal recognition. Ultimately, humility, sincerity, and a genuine dedication to God's word should be the driving forces behind a pastor's ministry.

Ultimately, it's a combination of the text and human interpretation that contributes to the diversity of denominations within Christianity and other religious groups. While it's important to respect and engage with different viewpoints, it's also crucial to approach discussions with humility, open-mindedness, and a spirit of understanding.

As believers, we often find ourselves divided over various issues. This leads to division within the body of Christ. Division can manifest in different ways. It can occur when we focus on our individual preferences and desires rather than the greater vision and purpose of the church. We may disagree on matters of worship styles, doctrinal interpretations, or even leadership decisions, which then result in divisions and factions within the body.

One reason for division among believers is the temptation to elevate our personal opinions above the teachings of scripture. We must remember that the Word of God is our ultimate authority, and our interpretations should be consistent with its teachings. When we allow our biases and preferences to drive our beliefs and actions, we set ourselves up for division.

Another mistake that leads to division is the failure to engage in healthy dialogue and constructive communication. Instead of seeking understanding and finding common ground, we tend to defend our positions rigidly and without an open mind. This lack of willingness to listen and communicate can widen the gap between believers and prevent unity within the body of Christ.

Additionally, division can also arise from a lack of humility and love. When we prioritize our own interests and desires above those of others, we create an environment that fosters division. Instead, we should strive to emulate the humility and love of Christ, who willingly laid down His life for His followers.

Promoting unity in the body of Christ requires intentional effort. First, we must recognize that unity does not mean uniformity. We can celebrate our differences and respect diverse perspectives while still maintaining unity in our common faith. Unity is not about conforming to a single way of thinking but about uplifting the core principles and values that unite us as believers.

Second, it is essential to cultivate an environment of grace and forgiveness. We need to extend grace to one another, acknowledging that we are all imperfect and prone to mistakes. When conflicts arise, instead of harboring grudges or holding onto past hurts, we should be quick to forgive and seek reconciliation.

Furthermore, promoting unity requires active participation in building relationships with other believers. It is through genuine relationships that we can understand one another's perspectives, find common ground, and work toward greater unity. We should be intentional about engaging in fellowship, attending church activities, and seeking opportunities to serve alongside our brothers and sisters in Christ.

In conclusion, the mistake of division is a significant hindrance to the unity of the body of Christ. By recognizing and addressing the factors that contribute to division, we can promote unity within the church. It is our responsibility as believers to value the greater vision and purpose of the body of Christ over our own preferences, engage in healthy dialogue and communication, and cultivate an environment of grace and forgiveness. May we all strive to promote unity in the body of Christ for the glory of God and the advancement of His kingdom.

CHAPTER SEVEN

THE MISTAKE OF NEGLECTING PERSONAL HOLINESS: PURSUING A GODLY CHARACTER

I n today's society, the pursuit of personal holiness and godly character is often overlooked or dismissed as unnecessary. Many people prioritize success, wealth, and material possessions over cultivating a righteous and godly lifestyle.

However, neglecting personal holiness is a grave mistake that can have far-reaching consequences.

Personal holiness, also known as sanctification, is the process of becoming more like Christ and conforming to God's standards of righteousness. It involves cultivating virtues such as love, humility, patience, and self-control while abstaining from sinful behaviors. Neglecting personal holiness means neglecting our relationship with God and failing to live up to the purpose He has for our lives.

One of the primary reasons why people neglect personal holiness is the belief that it is not essential for salvation. Many individuals view salvation as a one-time event, where they accept Jesus as their Savior and believe that is enough. While belief in Jesus is crucial for salvation, personal holiness is necessary for a transformed and authentic Christian life.

The Bible repeatedly emphasizes the importance of personal holiness. In (1 Peter 1:15-16), it says, "But just as he who called you is holy, so be holy in all you do; for it is written: 'Be holy because I am holy.'" God calls His people to reflect His holiness through their actions, thoughts, and attitudes.

Neglecting personal holiness is a direct contradiction to this call.

Another reason for neglecting personal holiness is the belief that Christians are under grace and, therefore, no longer bound by the law. While it is true that we are not justified by the works of the law, the grace of God should not be used as an excuse for sin or disobedience. In (Romans 6:1-2), the apostle Paul addresses this misconception, saying, "What shall we say, then? Shall we go on sinning so that grace may increase? By no means! We are those who have died to sin; how can we live in it any longer?"

Personal holiness is not about legalism or trying to earn salvation through good works. It is about responding to God's grace by living a life that honors Him and reflects His character. It is an ongoing journey of transformation guided by the Holy Spirit. Neglecting personal holiness not only dishonors God but also robs believers of the abundant life and blessings that come from aligning their lives with His will.

Moreover, neglecting personal holiness hinders our witness to the world. The way we live our lives speaks louder than anything we say. If we claim to follow Christ but our actions do not align with His teachings, we become a stumbling block to others and hinder them from experiencing the transformative power of the Gospel.

Neglecting personal holiness is a mistake that can have dire significant consequences for our spiritual well-being and our testimony as Christians. Pursuing a godly character is not an option for believers; it is a vital aspect of our faith journey. It is through personal holiness that we draw closer to God, experience His transforming power, and reflect His character to the world. Let us not neglect the pursuit of personal holiness but embrace it wholeheartedly, seeking to grow in Christlikeness every day.

Character development is crucial in the pursuit of a godly life because it shapes who we are at our core and influences the actions and decisions we make. Developing a strong and virtuous character rooted in the teachings of God helps us align our lives with His will and live in a way that reflects His values.

In the pursuit of a godly life, character development involves cultivating qualities such as love, compassion, humility, patience, forgiveness, and integrity. These virtues help us build healthy relationships, make ethical choices, and navigate life's challenges with grace and wisdom.

Character development also plays a vital role in our spiritual growth. By striving to embody the fruits of the Spirit - love, joy, peace, patience, kindness, goodness, faithfulness, gentleness, and self-control - we become more attuned to God's presence in our lives and are better equipped to fulfill His purpose for us.

Moreover, a well-developed character serves as a powerful witness to others, showcasing the transformative power of God's love and truth in our lives. Through our actions and interactions, we can inspire others to seek after God and pursue a life of righteousness and faith.

Ultimately, character development in the pursuit of a godly life is an ongoing process that requires self-reflection, humility, prayer, and a willingness to be molded by God's Word. As we continually strive to grow in character and deepen our relationship with God, we draw closer to Him and experience the abundant life He desires for us.

Developing a godly character is a noble pursuit that requires conscious effort and perseverance. However, there are several challenges and pitfalls that individuals may face on this journey. Some of these obstacles include:

1. Lack of Discipline: Developing a godly character requires consistent discipline and self-control. Without these qualities, it can be challenging to resist temptations and make choices that align with God's values.

2. Peer Influence: The influence of friends, colleagues, or society can sometimes lead individuals away from developing a godly character. Peer pressure to conform to worldly standards and values can sabotage efforts to grow spiritually.

3. Selfishness and Pride: The desires for power, recognition, and material possessions can hinder the development of a godly character. Pride can also lead to a lack of humility and compassion, which are essential traits for a godly character.

4. Unforgiveness and Bitterness: Holding onto grudges and resentments can poison the heart and prevent the growth of a godly character. Forgiveness and letting go of past hurts are crucial for spiritual growth.

5. Distractions and Busyness: In today's fast-paced world, distractions and busyness can prevent individuals from ded-

icating time to spiritual practices such as prayer, meditation, and studying scripture. Prioritizing God and His teachings is essential for developing a godly character.

6. <u>Lack of Accountability</u>: Without accountability from mentors, friends, or a faith community, individuals may struggle to stay on track in their pursuit of a godly character. Having a support system can provide encouragement, guidance, and correction when needed.

7. <u>Spiritual Dryness</u>: Periods of spiritual dryness or doubt can test an individual's faith and commitment to developing a godly character. It's essential to seek spiritual nourishment during these times through prayer, worship, and fellowship.

Overcoming these challenges and pitfalls requires intentional effort, reliance on God's strength, and a willingness to grow and change. Developing a godly character is a lifelong journey that requires humility, perseverance, and a sincere desire to reflect God's love and grace in all aspects of life.

CHAPTER EIGHT

THE MISTAKE OF MISINTERPRETING SCRIPTURE: ACCURATELY UNDERSTANDING GOD'S WORD

I n our journey to accurately understand God's Word, one of the biggest mistakes we can make is misinterpreting Scripture. Misinterpreting Scripture can lead us astray and cause confusion and conflict among believers. Therefore, it is crucial to approach the Bible with humility, seeking the guidance of the Holy Spirit and diligently studying the context and original intent of the passages.

A common mistake in misinterpreting Scripture is taking verses out of context. When we cherry-pick verses without considering the surrounding verses, we risk distorting the intended meaning. Each verse is part of a larger narrative, and it is vital to understand the flow of the passage and how it contributes to the overall message.

Misinterpreting Scripture can also occur when we impose our own biases and preconceived notions onto the text. It is essential to be aware of our own cultural, social, and personal influences that may cloud our understanding. We must approach the Bible with an open mind and allow the text to speak for itself rather than trying to fit it into our own agenda or beliefs.

Another mistake is failing to consider the original historical and cultural context of the passage. The Bible was written in a specific time and place, and understanding the customs, traditions, and language of that era can provide valuable insights into the meaning. Consulting commentaries, dictionaries, and other resources can help us gain a deeper understanding of the original context.

Furthermore, misinterpreting Scripture can occur when we neglect the use of sound hermeneutical principles. Hermeneutics is the study of interpretation, and it provides us with guidelines to accurately understand the Bible. These principles include considering the genre of the passage (whether it is historical, poetic, prophetic, etc.), understanding the author's intended audience, and interpreting difficult passages in light of clearer ones.

To avoid misinterpreting Scripture, it is essential to develop a disciplined study habit. This includes reading the Bible regularly, meditating on its teachings, and seeking guidance from trusted teachers and mentors. It is also helpful to engage in group Bible studies where we can learn from one another and encourage each other in our understanding of God's Word.

Ultimately, accurately understanding God's Word requires humility, diligent study, and reliance on the Holy Spirit's guidance. By avoiding the mistake of misinterpreting Scripture, we can grow in our knowledge of God and experience the transformative power of His Word in our lives.

Some people misinterpret Scripture for financial gain and control. Unfortunately, this is also how cults are formed. God never intended His word to be used as a weapon against us, but that's what Satan does. Satan attempts to pervert every good thing that has created us, including one another. Study the Bible for yourself so that you are not led astray, and ask God for understanding.

Here are some principles to keep in mind:

1. **Personal Study**:

- **(2 Timothy 2:15)** encourages us: "Do your best to present yourself to God as one approved, a worker who has no need to be ashamed, rightly handling the word of truth."

- Engage in personal Bible study, seeking God's wisdom and guidance.

1. **Avoiding Misinterpretation**:

- **(2 Peter 3:16)** warns about misinterpreting Scripture: "His letters contain some things that are hard to understand, which ignorant and unstable people distort, as they do the other Scriptures, to their own destruction."

- Be cautious of twisting Scripture to fit personal agendas.

1. **Prayer for Understanding**:

- **(James 1:5)** encourages us to seek wisdom: "If any of you lacks wisdom, let him ask God, who gives generously to all without reproach, and it will be given him."

- Pray for insight and understanding as you read the Bible.

1. **Context Matters**:

- Consider the **context** of each passage. Understand who wrote it, to whom, and why.

- Avoid cherry-picking verses out of context.

1. **Spiritual Discernment**:

- **(1 Corinthians 2:14)** reminds us: "The natural person does not accept the things of the Spirit of God, for they are folly to him, and he is not able to understand them because they are spiritually discerned."

- Rely on the Holy Spirit for discernment.

1. **Beware of False Teachers**:

- **(Matthew 7:15)** warns: "Beware of false prophets, who come to you in sheep's clothing but inwardly are ravenous wolves."

- Test teachings against Scripture and be wary of those who manipulate it for personal gain.

CHAPTER NINE

THE MISTAKE OF MATERIALISM: PUTTING GOD FIRST IN FINANCES AND POSSESSIONS

In a world dominated by consumerism and materialism, it's easy to fall into the trap of putting our finances and possessions ahead of our spirituality. However, this can lead us down a path of emptiness and disillusionment. In this chapter, we will explore the importance of putting God first in our finances and possessions, and the mistake of prioritizing material wealth over spiritual growth.

One of the key teachings of many spiritual traditions is the idea of detachment from material possessions. This does not mean we cannot enjoy the blessings of wealth and abundance, but rather that we should not let them control us. When we place too much importance on money and possessions, we lose sight of our spiritual purpose and connection to God.

In the Bible, Jesus famously said, "You cannot serve both God and money." This serves as a reminder that our ultimate allegiance should be to God, not to material wealth. When we prioritize God in our finances, we are guided by principles of generosity, stewardship, and compassion. We are called to use our resources to serve others and further the kingdom of God, rather than hoarding them for our own gain.

Putting God first in our finances also means trusting in His provision and guidance. We are called to be wise stewards of the resources God has given us, using them in ways that honor Him and benefit others. This requires faith and a willingness to let go of our sense of control, recognizing that God is ultimately in control of our financial well-being.

When we prioritize God in our finances and possessions, we experience a sense of freedom and peace that transcends material wealth. We no longer feel the pressure to keep up with societal expectations or accumulate more and more wealth. Instead, we find contentment in knowing that our true worth lies in our relationship with God, not in our bank accounts.

Ultimately, the mistake of materialism lies in the belief that our happiness and security can be found in the accumulation of wealth and possessions. True fulfillment comes from a deep connection to God and a willingness to let go of our attachment to worldly goods. By putting God first in our finances and possessions, we open ourselves up to a life of abundance, joy, and spiritual growth.

I would be doing this chapter a disservice if I didn't address tithing... ah, so many churches teach this in error. I know why, and deep down, many of you do, too; even non-believers know. I believe all the preachers in the world think and agree on the interpretation of the scripture (Malachi 3:10); well, at least 99.9 percent of them do. It's because you don't mess with the money, honey. The Church is so fearful about its own finances that many preach this in error and don't want to know the truth, or it overlooks it entirely. Welcome to the world of Churches Inc. and the Ten Percent Christian (my next book, perhaps).

So, without further ado, here's the truth. First, ponder and see if you can answer this question. Did you know that in the Old Testament, there were three tithes? Another question: ask yourself why the church only focuses on 10 percent tithing in general and never mentions the other two. The things that make you go, hmmm. Let's dive right into the three different tithes:

1. **The Levitical tithe**: This tithe was given by the Israelites to support the Levites, who were the tribe set apart for full-time service in the Tabernacle or temple. The Levites had no land inheritance of their own, so the tithe provided for their needs.

2. **The Festival tithe**: In addition to the Levitical tithe, the Israelites were also required to set aside a second tithe for the annual religious festivals and feasts. This tithe was used to celebrate and worship God as a community.

3. **The Poor tithe**: Every third year, the Israelites were to set aside a tithe to support the poor, widows, orphans, and foreigners living among them. This tithe helped ensure that those in need were cared for and provided for by the community.

The concept of tithing in ancient Israel differed significantly from the modern understanding of tithing as primarily involving monetary contributions. In the Old Covenant, tithing consisted of offering crops and produce as tithes. This included tithing grains, fruits, new wine, and oil each year.

The initial offspring of their livestock (Leviticus 27:30-33) could be exchanged for money if the designated place for tithing was too distant for the nation of Israel to transport their goods, like Jerusalem. The owner could then use the funds received in exchange to purchase any desired items, such as cattle, sheep, or wine (Deuteronomy).

According to (Deuteronomy 14:22-26), every third year, the tithe was set aside as a festival tithe. During this time, all the tithe and produce were gathered, and the Levite, the stranger, the orphan, the widow, and the poor in the town were invited to come and partake in a feast, ensuring they were well-fed and satisfied (Deuteronomy 14:28-29; 26:12-15).

I anticipate that those who promote tithing as a mandatory practice may not adhere to the third-year tithe requirement or the festival tithe.

Few scriptures have been more widely quoted than (Malachi 3:10), which says, "Bring the full tithe into the storehouse, that there may be food in my house. Test me in this," says the Lord Almighty, "and see if I will not throw open the floodgates of heaven and pour out so much blessing that there will not be room enough to store it."

The passage in (Malachi 3:10) has often been misinterpreted as a promise of God's blessing, specifically in terms of material wealth. However, a closer examination of the verse within its context reveals that it is not associated with financial prosperity. This terminology has historical roots, as seen in (Genesis 7:11), where God opened the windows of heaven.

The flood was caused by rain pouring down and the fountains of the deep breaking open. (Genesis 8:2) states that the windows of heaven were closed, and the rain stopped falling. Similarly, (Isaiah 24:18) references the windows from on high, a phrase often associated with water.

In (Malachi 3:10), God's judgment was seen as a blessing on their crops. The nation's livelihood revolved around agriculture, and they relied on rain for their sustenance. God's blessing was tied to His provision of water; without rain, they would face starvation. Giving God their tithes was a crucial part of receiving this blessing.

In the Mosaic covenant, if the people disobeyed God, He would impose a curse on them. The land's productivity would suffer as God would withhold rain, causing the ground to yield little food.

The ancient practice of tithing in Israel, following the Law of Moses, was a way for the nation to express trust in God and recognize His ownership of all things. However, the specific tithing laws outlined in the Mosaic code mostly involved agricultural produce, making it impractical to follow them in the modern context. Despite this, some still advocate for strict adherence to these tithing laws as an act of obedience. It's essential to understand that tithing in that context was more akin to paying taxes rather than giving voluntary gifts.

Tithes were given in addition to a variety of offerings, totaling more than 22% instead of just 10%. According to the law, giving only 10% of your tithes would still be considered stealing from God. One portion of the tithe was designated to provide for the Levites (Numbers 18:21-32), who were prohibited from owning property.

Other tribes of Israel also contributed to the Levitical priests, providing them with a tithe that encompassed not only money but also goods. These offerings sustained the Levites in their service at the Tabernacle, allowing them to support themselves. In return, the Levites were instructed to tithe a portion of the goods they received and dedicate it back to the community.

The duty of tithing a tenth to the high priest's office is outlined in (Numbers 18:21-28). The Levites were responsible for bringing this tithe to the storehouse chambers in the house of God, as mentioned in (Nehemiah 10:38). The passage in Malachi is often cited as proof for tithing, but it is not a rebuke, as many believe.

In (1 Timothy 1:5-7), the writer is admonishing the Levites for hoarding the tithe meant for them. Today, when prosperity preachers urge their followers to be faithful using this verse, they are inadvertently indicting themselves. Their lack of biblical understanding prevents them from grasping the true message behind the rebuke.

The commandment intends to encourage love that stems from a pure heart, a good conscience, and sincere faith. However, some have wandered from this path and have become engrossed in frivolous chatter. They aspire to be authorities on the law but lack understanding of the subjects they discuss or affirm.

In the New Testament, the concept of grace-filled giving differs from the obligatory tithing outlined in the laws given to Israel by Moses. While tithing was mandatory for the nation of Israel under God's command, there is no such requirement specified in the New Testament for Christians. The emphasis in the New Testament is on giving joyfully and according to one's own discretion, rather than being bound by a set percentage of income.

Advocates of tithing in the prosperity movement often cite Jesus' emphasis on tithing in the New Testament. While the concept of tithing is mentioned eight times in the New Testament, it is in reference to the Old Testament laws. During Jesus' time, tithing was still observed as a religious practice, but Jesus' own mention of tithing was a criticism of the Pharisees for prioritizing rituals over justice and love.

Jesus highlighted the importance of justice, mercy, and faith in addition to tithing, emphasizing that the Pharisees were neglecting these essential aspects of a faithful life. This critique of the Pharisees revealed their lack of fairness and compassion towards others, as depicted in the story of the Pharisee and the tax collector. Jesus taught that humility and mercy were key components of a true relationship with God, not just adherence to religious practices.

It is evident that merely giving is insufficient to attain justification before God. Nevertheless, a considerable number of individuals have come to believe that their obedience to giving is the key to receiving blessings from God.

The Pharisees claimed to have faith, but their true interest lay in money. Jesus pointed out that they were lovers of money, and they mocked Him. As Jesus scolded them, He revealed that what society values is detestable to God. He then shared a parable about the rich man and Lazarus. In the parable, the poor man found solace in Abraham's embrace among the faithful, while the rich man found himself in torment. The rich man's punishment was not due to his wealth but because he was self-centered and indifferent to the suffering of poor Lazarus, whom he ignored daily as he sat by his gate.

What are the most significant aspects of the law that Christians should prioritize? Giving to those in need should be the main focus. "The second is like this, 'You shall love your neighbor as yourself.' There is no other commandment greater than these" (Mark 12:31; Galatians 5:14). "Bear one another's burdens, and in this way, you will fulfill the law of Christ" (Galatians 6:2). The main principle is to assist others, particularly the less fortunate brethren, aligning with the teachings of (Deuteronomy 14:26).

Those who advocate for tithing often rely on the Old Covenant law to support their belief in this method of receiving blessings. Prosperity teachers are known to shift people away from grace and into legalistic practices to line their pockets. They take people's love for God and use it against them in error; this is the greatest mind trick and play on emotions that the world has ever seen. In the New Testament, there is no fixed amount mandated for giving; rather, individuals are encouraged to give as they can willingly and cheerfully. As it says, "Each one should give what he has proposed in his own heart, for God loves a cheerful giver."

In the New Testament, there is no specific requirement for tithing mentioned by Paul or any other apostle. In contrast, the nation of Israel was obligated to tithe under the Old Testament law as they were a theocratic nation. Before His crucifixion, Jesus adhered to the law and even had Peter pay the temple tax. However, with the establishment of the New Covenant after Jesus' crucifixion, the Old Covenant was fulfilled. New Testament Christians were not bound by the Old Covenant law, and tithing is not explicitly mandated, like the observance of the Lord's Supper and Baptism.

There are no epistles that chastise individuals for failing to tithe, but the importance of giving with a generous and supportive attitude is emphasized. Having God's blessings does not require tithing, and those who are wealthy are encouraged to be humble, trust in God, and generously share their resources to enrich others and build a foundation for eternal life.

In today's society, there is a common desire among the poor to become rich, while the rich often perceive themselves as blessed and view their wealth as an indicator of their spiritual well-being. However, this focus on material abundance can lead to spiritual bankruptcy, as Jesus warned in the Scriptures. The church of Laodicea serves as an example of those who have fallen into this trap. Recall the scripture, where Christ says in (Matthew 19:24), "Again, I tell you, it's easier for a camel to pass through the eye of a needle than it is for a rich man to enter the kingdom of Heaven, but with God all things are possible."

It is important to remember Jesus' teachings about money, which often included warnings and rebukes rather than promises of wealth for His followers. Despite the prevalent prosperity preaching of today, Jesus emphasized the dangers of covetousness and highlighted that a person's true value is not measured by their possessions.

Throughout the Bible, we are cautioned against the pursuit of riches and reminded that true blessings come from faithfulness to the Lord, regardless of one's material wealth. Solomon, a man who possessed great riches, also recognized the pitfalls of hastening after wealth and neglecting spiritual matters.

Ultimately, we are called to be content with what we have, understanding that our true provision comes from God through Christ. It is not simply the accumulation of material blessings, as the world views it, which defines our worth, but our commitment to spiritual life and faithful service to the Lord.

It is challenging to determine the exact origins of the legalistic requirement of tithing within the Church, but its current popularity can be attributed to modern prosperity teachers who promote seed faith giving. Some teachers use (Mark 10:30) to promise that whatever is given to the Lord will be multiplied one hundred times, but Jesus was actually referring to leaving possessions and relationships to follow Him. Did you know there would have been a 13th disciple? Recall the rich man who wanted to follow Jesus, and he asked Jesus what was needed on his end to follow Him, and Jesus told him to sell everything he owned and give it to the poor (Mark 10:21-22). Sadly, the rich man was not willing to go that far to follow Jesus.

The concept of money and giving is not directly mentioned in association with the hundredfold in Mark. It is concerning to see some teachers manipulating congregations towards a culture of coveting through their teachings on giving. It is important to carefully examine the passage and consider the motivations behind those promoting such interpretations. Solomon's words in (Proverbs 30:15), "The leech has two daughters--give and Give!" serve as a reminder to be wary of those who only seek to be on the receiving end.

Some individuals assert that tithing is the sole way to support the local church and believe one's spirituality is determined by tithing to the church. Some have even gone to the extreme of suggesting that tithing is necessary for salvation, claiming that those who do not give 10% are not genuine Christians. Unfortunately, lying and manipulation also exist in the Church, as they do in politics. Woe to those who knowingly preach and teach in error.

Some teachings suggest that failure to tithe will result in being cursed, employing more manipulation tactics. The book of Malachi is often cited, with a focus on chapter 3, but for a broader understanding, one should also consider (Malachi 4:4), which mentions "Remember the Law of Moses." This implies that tithing is just one aspect of the Law.

However, choosing to adhere to any part of the Law of Moses means one is bound by the entire law, as stated in (Galatians 3:10). This contradicts the idea that solely tithing under obligation is sufficient. According to (Galatians 5:4), relying on the law for justification nullifies the grace provided by Christ.

If you are facing financial challenges that are preventing you from providing for your family or meeting your mortgage obligations, remember that you are not required to give 10% of your income to the church. As the Apostle Paul stated in (1 Timothy 5:8), "But if anyone does not provide for their relatives, and especially for their own household, they have denied the faith and are worse than an unbeliever." Taking care of your family is your primary responsibility; you can be confident that the church will manage without your financial contribution.

If you have money set aside for your family's needs, it is important to prioritize using it for them rather than diverting it to a church or ministry as tithes or offerings. Paying off your debts should not come at the expense of your family's well-being. Avoid falling for schemes that promise unrealistic financial gains in exchange for donations, as they may exploit your vulnerabilities and fuel your greed.

Remember to be mindful of your responsibilities to both your loved ones and to God. Scripture does not endorse giving beyond your means or treating donations as a transaction with divine rewards. Let us be cautious of those who prioritize monetary gain over genuine faith and service, as their motives may not align with the teachings of Jesus. Ultimately, our actions should reflect a sincere devotion to God, free from the temptations of material wealth.

If your family is struggling with hunger and rent, you should not feel obligated to tithe to the church. Instead, the church should willingly offer assistance, as helping those in need is fundamental to their purpose. This is exemplified in the early church (Acts 4:37) and driven by the love of Christ (2 Corinthians 5:14). God's heart is to provide for the needy, even through financial means. The church should actively seek opportunities to support those less fortunate rather than those who are already well-off. It is disheartening to hear stories of ministries receiving prolonged support while individuals in distress are left without help.

Is your motivation purely legalistic or from the heart? As Christians, we are called to emulate the love of Jesus by reaching out and meeting the needs of others. Love should guide our actions, not just following rules. Even if we give everything we have to the poor, without love, it is meaningless (1 Corinthians 13:3). Giving should stem from a genuine desire to help, not merely as an obligation. This is not a cheerful giver.

Jesus emphasized the importance of helping the less fortunate over giving to His ministry. In (Luke 12:33-34), He taught us to sell possessions, give to the needy, and store up treasures in heaven. Zacchaeus demonstrated an understanding of this principle by declaring his intent to give half of his wealth to the poor and make amends for any wrongs he had committed. Jesus commended him, noting that salvation had come to his household. The message is clear - true blessings come from giving selflessly to those in need out of a genuine heart rather than seeking personal gain.

It is important to refrain from endorsing false teachers and those who seek to exploit both money and the gospel for their personal gain. Rather, our support should be directed towards individuals who exhibit sincerity and are genuinely in need of assistance in their work for the Lord. Those who are dedicated to full-time ministry should be sustained by the very community they serve (1 Corinthians 9:7-14; 1 Timothy 5:17-18), while those engaged in ministry and missions require backing from those who remain at home and possess resources.

A thorough examination of New Testament practices on giving indicates that our financial contributions should not only aid our local churches and ministries but also address the essential needs of our fellow believers (Acts 2:44-45, 4:32-37; 1 Corinthians 16:1-3; 2 Corinthians 8:1-13; 1 Timothy 6:17-19). Local assemblies were deliberate in their provision for widows and orphans within the faith community who lacked other sources of support (Acts 6:1-4; 1 Timothy 5:1-16).

There is no mention of tithing in the early Church as depicted in the book of Acts. In (Acts 4:32-37), wealthy Christians sold their assets and gave the proceeds to the Apostles for the benefit of the Christian community in need, not for the Apostles themselves. The Apostles then distributed the funds as needed. The singular instance concerning money in Acts is found in (Acts 5:1-11), where Ananias and Sapphira were condemned for dishonesty. They were censured for retaining a portion of the money from the sale of their land, which they had pledged to give in full, unlike everyone else. This incident was not related to tithing but rather to the importance of being truthful and honoring one's commitments.

(Proverbs 22:16) warns against oppressing the poor in pursuit of wealth, stating that those who give to the rich will inevitably face poverty. Unfortunately, some prosperity teachers exploit this message by making false promises of prosperity to the less fortunate in exchange for financial contributions. This goes against biblical principles, as God has always emphasized caring for the poor, homeless, fatherless, and widowed.

In today's society, the neglect of these vulnerable groups is evident, especially among those who preach mandatory tithing. The practice of the third-year tithe, which was designed to provide food and support for the less fortunate, is often overlooked. It is crucial to reflect on how we treat the poor and needy, as it reflects our spiritual state.

The absence of invitations for the poor and needy to events funded by ministries raises questions about their commitment to serving those in need. This lack of consideration for the less fortunate contradicts the teachings of scripture and calls into question the sincerity of those who claim to follow them.

Our giving should be done willingly, joyfully, and out of a desire to make an offering. As Christians, we need to be generous by sharing our possessions with those in need and supporting legitimate Christian ministries. Each believer should contribute to the church they attend and support the local work being done in their community. Giving can also extend to missionaries, other ministries, or any other cause that resonates with them or is placed in their hearts by the Holy Spirit. While aiming to contribute around 10 percent of our income is a good target, the important thing is to give willingly and with a joyful heart, as emphasized in the New Testament. Tithing as a way to solve financial difficulties is not a Biblical practice but a misconception promoted by certain prosperity preachers. Instead, we should focus on being responsible with our finances and directing our support towards those truly in need of help for the advancement of God's work.

The New Testament challenges the concept of tithing as a doctrine when discussing giving. (2 Corinthians 9:7) emphasizes giving according to one's own heart and not out of obligation. The verse encourages giving joyfully and cheerfully, as God values a happy giver. The Greek word for cheerful, *hilaros*, is related to the English word "hilarious," suggesting giving in a joyful and exuberant manner. It emphasizes the importance of giving willingly and happily to support the expansion of God's Kingdom. On the contrary, giving grudgingly, marked by the Greek word *lupe*, which conveys feelings of sorrow and annoyance, is discouraged. If giving is done reluctantly, out of compulsion, or with a sense of obligation, it goes against the spirit of cheerful giving advocated in the New Testament.

The Apostle Paul emphasizes in (1 Corinthians 16:2) the importance of setting aside a portion on the first day of the week based on one's prosperity, allowing for generous giving without the need for collections upon his arrival. Contrary to the concept of tithing, giving should be a personal decision made in accordance with one's heart and prosperity level, with the freedom to choose the amount. God does not use pressure, guilt, or incentives to manipulate our giving, unlike the common practices seen elsewhere. It's worth noting that Jesus Himself did not solicit offerings during His ministry.

Love should be our driving force, not obligation or strict adherence to rules (refer to Hosea 6:6, Micah 6:6-8, Mark 12:28-34, and 1 Corinthians 13:1-7). The depth of a person's love for God is reflected in their desire to contribute to His work, which doesn't always involve financial donations.

Once again, it is important to acknowledge that ministries require support, but distorting the teachings of God to solicit support by promising extravagant blessings is deceptive. The focus should not be solely on money but rather on the intentions and motivations of the heart. Our relationship with money reveals our true priorities in God's eyes. Instead of seeking immediate rewards on earth, our gaze should be fixed on the eternal treasure awaiting us in heaven. Giving with the expectation of material gain is contrary to the essence of true generosity. Jesus emphasized the connection between our treasures and our hearts, highlighting the significance of our motives. It is crucial to give selflessly without seeking personal benefits in return.

We should rally behind those engaged in ministry, uphold the efforts of our churches, and actively seek out opportunities to lend a helping hand to those in need as directed by God.

I'll share this concluding reflection on wealth. It's intriguing that I've never encountered a pastor, preacher, or evangelical who has addressed the biblical verse asserting that no one should profit from God's word. Nevertheless, numerous individuals lead opulent lives at the Church's expense. No disciple or minister in the Bible lived extravagantly; they were not attached to worldly possessions and held reverence for God. Jesus worked as a carpenter, and Apostle Paul was a tent maker. It is audacious to speak of God and misrepresent Him simultaneously.

CHAPTER TEN

THE MISTAKE OF FAILING TO SHARE THE GOSPEL: SPREADING THE GOOD NEWS

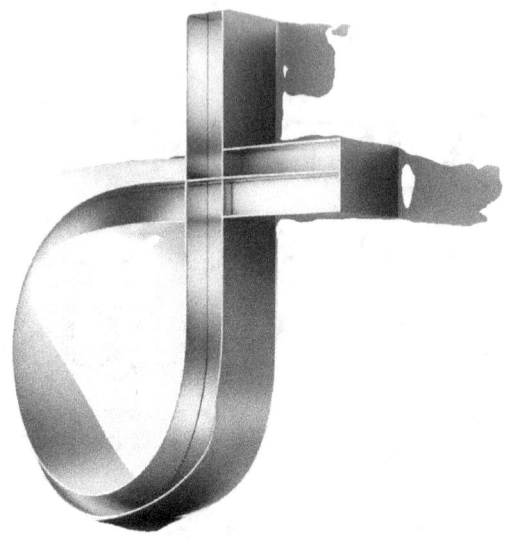

In this chapter, we will discuss the mistake of failing to share the gospel and the importance of spreading the good news. Sharing the gospel is a fundamental aspect of the Christian faith, yet many believers often neglect this crucial responsibility.

The gospel is the good news of salvation through faith in Jesus Christ. It is a message of hope, forgiveness, and eternal life.

As Christians, we have been commissioned by Jesus Himself to go and make disciples of all nations, baptizing them in the name of the Father, the Son, and the Holy Spirit.

However, due to various reasons such as fear, apathy, or a lack of understanding, many believers fail to share the gospel with others. This is a grave mistake as it goes against our calling as followers of Christ. We are called to be witnesses to Jesus, sharing His love and grace with others.

One reason why believers may fail to share the gospel is fear. Fear of rejection, criticism, or persecution can paralyze us and prevent us from fulfilling our role as ambassadors of Christ. However, we must remember that Jesus promised to be with us always, even to the end of the age. He will give us the courage and strength to overcome our fears and boldly proclaim His message.

Another reason for failing to share the gospel is a lack of concern or a lack of understanding. Some believers may not fully grasp the significance of the gospel or the urgency of sharing it. They may become complacent and comfortable in their own salvation, forgetting that there are countless souls in need of the good news. It is essential for believers to constantly remind themselves of the precious gift of salvation and the importance of sharing it with others.

The consequences of failing to share the gospel are severe. When we withhold the good news from those who are lost and searching for meaning in their lives, we deny them the opportunity to experience the transformative power of Jesus Christ. We rob them of the chance to have their sins forgiven and to be reconciled with God. Moreover, failing to share the gospel can have eternal repercussions. If people do not hear and respond to the message of salvation, they face the tragic consequence of eternal separation from God.

As believers, we must recognize the weightiness of our responsibility to share the gospel. We need to overcome our fears and step out in faith, knowing that God is with us. We should cultivate a burden for the lost, praying for opportunities to share the good news and allowing the Holy Spirit to guide and empower us in our evangelistic efforts.

Furthermore, we should equip ourselves with a solid understanding of the gospel and be able to communicate it effectively to others. This requires studying the Word of God, seeking the guidance of the Holy Spirit, and being prepared to give a reason for the hope that is in us.

Please understand the mistake of failing to share the gospel is a grave error that hinders the fulfillment of our calling as disciples of Jesus Christ. We must overcome our fears, apathy, and lack of understanding, and actively share the good news with others. Let us be obedient to Christ's command to make disciples of all nations, embracing the privilege and responsibility of spreading the gospel to the ends of the earth.

Consider this parable:

Once, there was a man named John who lived next door to a man named David. John knew that David didn't believe in Jesus Christ, but he was hesitant to share the gospel with him for fear of rejection or awkwardness. Days turned into weeks and then into years, and John never found the courage to speak to David about his faith.

One day, tragedy struck when David suddenly passed away from a heart attack. John was filled with regret and guilt, realizing that he had missed the opportunity to share the love of Christ with his neighbor. He felt like he had failed in his duty as a Christian to spread the good news of salvation.

However, when John spoke to David's wife after his passing, she revealed something unexpected. A few days before his death, a coworker shared the gospel with David, and he accepted Jesus as his savior. This revelation caught John off guard, feeling a mix of relief and sorrow.

He realized that while he had missed his chance to share the gospel with David, someone else had stepped in and led him to Christ. Despite his own failure, John found solace in the fact that God had used another person to bring salvation to his neighbor.

From then on, John vowed to never let fear or hesitation stop him from sharing the gospel with others. He learned that even when he falls short, God's plan and purpose prevail and that, ultimately, it is He who brings about salvation to those who seek it.

End of Parable

So, even though this was just a parable that I wrote, I'm sure this has happened somewhere in this world at some point in time. Every parable Jesus told was either real life or something that could actually happen in real life; that is the whole point of parables. I pray that we all find the courage to spread the gospel. I've found that God will always present the opportunity for us to do so, or He'll literally put it on your heart or flat-out tell you to give a word to someone specifically.

If spreading the gospel is difficult for you or you need some icebreaker ideas to do so, see the list below.

Spreading the good news of Jesus Christ can be done in a variety of ways, and different methods may work best for different people. Here are some suggestions:

1. **Live out your faith**: The most powerful testimony you can offer is through your actions and how you live out the teachings of Jesus Christ. Let your love, kindness, and compassion shine through in all your interactions with others.

2. **Share your personal story**: One of the most effective ways to share the good news is by sharing your own personal experience of how Jesus Christ has changed your life. People tend to respond well to authentic, personal stories.

3. **Invite others to church**: Encourage friends, family, and acquaintances to join you for a service at your church. This can be a non-threatening way for them to learn more about

the teachings of Jesus Christ and experience a community of believers.

4. **Use social media**: Share uplifting messages, Bible verses, and testimonies on your social media platforms. You can reach a wide audience and engage with people who may not have been open to discussing faith in person.

5. **Serve others**: Get involved in community service projects or volunteer opportunities that demonstrate the love of Christ through your actions. This can open up opportunities for conversations about your faith with those you serve alongside.

6. **Pray**: Above all, prayer is essential in sharing the good news of Jesus Christ. Pray for opportunities to share your faith, for the courage to speak up when the time is right, and for the hearts of those who may be receptive to the message.

Remember, the most important thing is to approach sharing the good news with humility, love, and respect for others' beliefs. It's ultimately up to the individual to accept or reject the message, but your role is to faithfully share it in a way that reflects the grace and love of Christ. One final thought on this: the Bible tells us that Jesus will not return until the gospel has been preached throughout the world, so let us get to it and spread the word of God.

(Matthew 24:14) says: "And this gospel of the kingdom will be proclaimed throughout the whole world as a testimony to all nations, and then the end will come."

Chapter Eleven

The Mistake of Neglecting Compassion

I want to start this chapter with a personal story. When I was around seven years old, I remember one particular morning when I was watching TV, and one of those Feed, the Children commercials came on and asked people to donate money for the starving children in Africa. I can't remember the exact amount they were asking people to donate, but I remember feeling compassion for these malnourished children with bugs and flies flying about their faces and seeing the despair in their eyes. So, I turned to my mom's boyfriend, Sam, and asked him if we could send in the money they were asking for because I didn't want those kids to go hungry. I must note that my family was not wealthy; we were poor and lived in a low-income apartment complex.

Sam pulls out all the money he has in his pocket and says, "Chubby (my nickname), we can send in this money to feed those kids, or we can take this money and go up to the corner market and buy us some food so we can have something to eat today." When Sam told me this, I pondered his question and felt hungry pains in my stomach. So, I told Sam, "We need to eat first before we can feed the kids in Africa." Sam smiled at me, and he agreed. I share this story because, as a child, I had the compassion to help the kids, but my family didn't have the means to do so.

In the gospel of Matthew, Jesus frequently confronts the Pharisees, criticizing them for their self-righteousness and lack of compassion. These religious leaders of Jesus' time were well-versed in following the laws and rituals, but they neglected the most crucial aspect of their faith: love and care for others.

Jesus often condemned the Pharisees for their judgmental attitude. They were quick to point out the faults and short-comings of others but failed to show any empathy or under-standing. They were so consumed with enforcing religious regulations that they disregarded the needs and struggles of the people around them.

The mistake the Pharisees made wasn't just a matter of for-getting to be compassionate; it was a conscious decision to prioritize their own righteousness over the well-being of their fellow human beings. They viewed themselves as superior and looked down upon those who didn't meet their stan-dards.

This attitude is also a warning to us today. It's easy to become so focused on our own faith practices or personal success that we forget to extend love and compassion to others. We might become judgmental, self-righteous, or indifferent to the needs of those around us.

But Jesus teaches us a different way. He models a radical and unconditional compassion. He reminds us that the greatest commandment is not to keep all the rules flawlessly, but to love God and love our neighbors as ourselves.

Compassion is not just a nice sentiment; it is an active response to the suffering and struggles of others. It requires us to see beyond ourselves and our own interests, open our hearts, and extend a helping hand to those in need. Compassion means not just feeling sorry for others but seeking to understand their pain and taking steps to alleviate it.

In the parable of the Good Samaritan, Jesus challenges His listeners to be like the compassionate Samaritan who stops to help a wounded stranger rather than the religious leaders who walk past. He calls us to be radically compassionate, willing to go out of our way to care for others, regardless of their background, beliefs, or social status.

Neglecting compassion is a mistake that we must be cautious of. We are called to be agents of love and care in the world, following the example of Jesus. As we navigate our lives, let us remember the importance of compassion and the detrimental consequences of neglecting it. May we not repeat the mistakes of the Pharisees but instead strive to love and care for others unconditionally.

In pursuing success and personal growth, it is easy to become consumed by our goals and ambitions. We often get caught up in the race to achieve and forget the importance of loving and caring for others. This neglect of compassion is a grave mistake that can hinder our overall happiness and fulfillment in life.

When we neglect compassion, we lose sight of our interconnectedness as human beings. We forget that each person we encounter is fighting their battles and facing their struggles. By failing to acknowledge this, we miss opportunities to show kindness and empathy, which can make a significant difference in someone's life.

Moreover, neglecting compassion affects our relationships. It can make us self-centered and insensitive, leading to strained connections with loved ones, friends, and colleagues. People are drawn to individuals who genuinely care about them, and when we neglect compassion, we risk losing those important bonds.

Loving and caring for others also promotes personal growth and development. It allows us to learn from different perspectives and experiences, broadening our horizons. Compassion encourages a sense of gratitude and humility, reminding us of how fortunate we are and urging us to pay it forward.

Practicing compassion can be as simple as lending a listening ear to a friend, offering a helping hand to someone in need, or showing kindness to a stranger. These small acts have the power to create ripple effects of positivity, not only in the lives of others but also in our own.

Furthermore, compassion is not solely about helping others—it also includes self-compassion. Taking care of ourselves is crucial to maintaining healthy emotional and mental well-being. When we neglect self-compassion, we may fall into the trap of self-criticism and neglect our own needs. By treating ourselves with kindness and understanding, we set the foundation for better relationships with others and a more fulfilling life.

In conclusion, neglecting compassion is a mistake that can have significant consequences. It hampers our ability to connect with others, damages our relationships, and hinders our personal growth. It is essential to prioritize loving and caring for others through acts of kindness towards them and by practicing self-compassion. By doing so, we enrich our own lives and create a positive impact on the world around us.

A simple act of kindness can be the difference between life and death for someone who is at the end of their rope, so to speak. Your act of kindness could be the spark of light a person needs to get help. We're called to be the light of the world, not the shadows of this world. So, I encourage you to speak up, stand up for the faith, and spread the love of Jesus.

Chapter Twelve

THE MISTAKE OF NEGLECTING PRAYER: EMBRACING THE POWER OF COMMUNICATION WITH GOD

I n today's reality, we often find ourselves caught up in the busyness of life. Work, family, responsibilities, and commitments can easily consume our time and energy. Unfortunately, in the midst of this chaos, we often neglect prayer, which is one of the most powerful tools we have at our disposal.

Prayer is more than just a religious ritual or meaningless words spoken into the void. It is a means of communication with God, a way to connect with the divine and seek guidance, comfort, and strength. Yet, many of us overlook this powerful resource, failing to realize the immense benefits that come from embracing the power of prayer.

One of the biggest mistakes we make is assuming that we can handle everything on our own. We live in a society that values self-sufficiency and independence, often encouraging us to rely solely on our own abilities. While it is important to take responsibility for our lives, we must also recognize our limitations. We are human, and there will be times when we need help and guidance that goes beyond our own capabilities.

Prayer allows us to tap into a higher power to seek wisdom and guidance from a source that is beyond our comprehension. Through prayer, we acknowledge that we are not alone and that God, as a divine presence, is always ready to listen and assist us. It is through this humble act of reaching out that we open ourselves up to a greater source of strength and wisdom.

Moreover, prayer is not just about asking for things or seeking solutions to our problems. It is also an act of surrender, a way to release our burdens and worries to the divine. When we pray, we acknowledge that we are not in control of everything and that there are forces at work beyond our understanding. This act of surrender brings us peace and serenity, knowing that we are not alone in our struggles.

Additionally, prayer is a means of gratitude. It allows us to express our appreciation for the blessings and goodness in our lives. By taking the time to acknowledge and thank God for all that we have, we cultivate a grateful heart, which in turn attracts more blessings into our lives. Prayer is a reminder to be present and mindful of the many gifts that surround us.

Furthermore, prayer is a way to cultivate a deeper spiritual connection. It is through this practice that we develop a relationship with God, a relationship built on trust, love, and faith. Just as relationships require communication and effort, so does our relationship with the divine. Prayer becomes a way to nurture and strengthen this bond, allowing us to experience a sense of peace, love, and belonging.

Neglecting prayer is a mistake that many of us make in our busy lives. However, by embracing the power of communication with God, we open ourselves up to immense benefits. Prayer allows us to seek guidance, find solace in times of adversity, cultivate gratitude, and deepen our spiritual connection. It is through prayer that we can experience the power of divine intervention in our lives, bringing us peace, strength, and a sense of purpose. So, let us not overlook this powerful tool and instead embrace prayer as an integral part of our daily lives.

We've often heard over the years, whether in a movie, TV show, or mostly in our lives shared with friends and family, this coined phrase of desperation, "Well, there is nothing else that we can do now but pray." When I hear this, it saddens me and makes me angry at times because Christians truly don't understand the power of prayer. Prayer is not the last line of defense; prayer is not waving the white flag of surrender, but prayer should be the first line of offense. As Christians, we have weapons to use at our disposal, and prayer is their pinnacle.

We should pray about every single thing that is going on or taking up space in our lives. Let God be your best friend, and let His heart be your dairy. Give all your woes, desires, successes, and failures to the Almighty. He can bear it all, but we simply cannot. Prayer is a powerful thing, and that is why God tells us to pray without ceasing. We desperately need it at every moment of our lives, so much that we don't understand, and I believe we truly don't know how wickedness surrounds us here on Earth. There are many evils that we can't see in the physical. So, I'll leave you with some scriptures showing how prayer was used as a spiritual weapon.

1. **(Ephesians 6:18)** - "And pray in the Spirit on all occasions with all kinds of prayers and requests. With this in mind, be alert and always keep on praying for all the Lord's people."

2. **(2 Corinthians 10:4-5)** - "The weapons we fight with are not the weapons of the world. On the contrary, they have the divine power to demolish strongholds. We demolish arguments and every pretension that sets itself up against

the knowledge of God, and we take captive every thought to make it obedient to Christ."

3. (James 5:16) - "Therefore confess your sins to each other and pray for each other so that you may be healed. The prayer of a righteous person is powerful and effective."

4. (Philippians 4:6-7) - "Do not be anxious about anything, but in every situation, by prayer and petition, with thanksgiving, present your requests to God. And the peace of God, which transcends all understanding, will guard your hearts and your minds in Christ Jesus."

5. The Prayer of Jabez (1 Chronicles 4:10) - Jabez prayed for God to bless him, enlarge his territory, be with him, and keep him from harm. This prayer emphasizes seeking God's favor and protection.

These verses emphasize the importance and effectiveness of prayer as a spiritual weapon in the life of a believer.

Many of us are struggling and need peace in our lives. Consider these ten short but powerful prayers:

1. "God, grant me the serenity to accept the things I cannot change, courage to change the things I can, and wisdom to know the difference. May peace flow into every area of my life."

2. "Lord, calm the storms in my heart and mind. Let your peace reign in every situation, bringing me tranquility and harmony."

3. "Heavenly Father, instill in me a spirit of forgiveness and understanding. Help me let go of anger and resentment, replacing them with peace and love."

4. "God of peace, guide me through moments of uncertainty and turmoil. Grant me the strength to remain grounded in your peace, no matter the circumstances."

5. "Lord, may your peace be a constant presence in my life, enveloping me in a sense of calm and security. Let your peace fill every corner of my being."

6. "Divine Creator, help me find peace within myself, knowing that I am loved and accepted just as I am. May this inner peace radiate outwards to bring harmony to all aspects of my life."

7. "God, grant me the courage to seek peace in times of conflict, the patience to listen and understand others, and the grace to forgive. Let peace be the guiding force in all my interactions."

8. "Lord, I surrender my worries and fears to you, trusting in your divine plan. Fill me with your peace that surpasses all understanding, bringing a sense of calm and assurance to my soul."

9. "Heavenly Father, remove any barriers that stand in the way of peace in my life. Fill me with your light and love, allowing me to walk in peace and harmony each day."

10. "God, bless me with the gift of peace, that I may be a source of tranquility and hope to those around me. Let your peace flow through me, bringing unity and healing wherever I go."

Payers For Healing:

1. Heavenly Father, I come to you in prayer, asking for your divine intervention in healing my body, mind, and spirit. Please grant me the strength and courage to overcome this illness, and restore me to full health and vitality. In Jesus' Name, Amen.

2. Lord Jesus, you are the ultimate healer. I humbly ask for your healing touch to be upon me, bringing comfort and relief from pain and suffering. May your love and power flow through me, restoring me to wellness and wholeness. In Jesus' Name, Amen.

3. Holy Spirit, I invite your healing presence into my life, filling me with peace and renewal. Remove any obstacles to my well-being and grant me the grace to embrace healing at every level. May your healing energy surround me and bring about miracles in my body, mind, and soul. In Jesus' Name, Amen.

4. Sacred Source of all life, I surrender myself to your healing light and wisdom. Guide me on the path to wellness, showing me the way to physical, emotional, and spiritual restoration. Fill me with your healing grace and love, bringing about a miraculous transformation in my being. In Jesus' Name, Amen.

5. Divine Physician, I place my trust in your infinite power to heal me. Be with me in my time of need, granting me strength and resilience to overcome any illness or affliction. May your healing energy flow through me, rejuvenating every cell and restoring balance to my body, mind, and spirit. In Jesus' name, Amen.

Payers For Blessings:

1. Heavenly Father, I come before you today with a humble heart and a grateful spirit. I thank you for all the blessings you have bestowed upon me thus far, and I pray that you continue to shower me with your grace and favor. Grant me the strength to face any challenges that come my way, and guide me toward the path of righteousness. May your divine light shine upon me and lead me to prosperity and abundance. In Jesus' Name, Amen.

2. O Lord, I seek your blessing and protection in all areas of my life. Help me to remain steadfast in my faith and to always choose love and kindness in all that I do. Bless me with good health, financial stability, and harmonious relationships with others. Grant me the wisdom and resilience to overcome any obstacles that may stand in my way. May your divine presence be felt in every aspect of my life, bringing peace, joy, and abundance. In Jesus' Name, Amen.

3. Dear God, I offer up this prayer for your divine blessings to pour down upon me like rain. May your love and grace surround me and uplift me in times of need. Bless me with a heart full of compassion, a mind filled with wisdom, and a spirit guided by faith. Grant me the strength to walk in your ways and the courage to follow your will. I am grateful for all that you have given me, and I humbly ask for your continued blessings to fill my life with abundance and fulfillment. In Jesus' Name, Amen.

These prayers can be personalized and adapted to suit your individual needs and circumstances.

A Prayer for Our Children:

Dear Heavenly Father, we come before you now with hearts full of love and concern for our children. We ask for your guidance, protection, and blessings upon them as they navigate the challenges of life.

We pray that you watch over them, keeping them safe from harm and danger. Give them the wisdom to make good decisions and the strength to resist temptation. Surround them with positive influences that will help them grow into the amazing individuals you have created them to be.

Lord, we ask for your provision in every aspect of their lives - physically, emotionally, mentally, and spiritually. May they experience your unfailing love and grace in abundance, knowing that they are cherished and cherished by you.

Help us, as parents, to be a shining example of your love and mercy to our children. Give us the patience, wisdom, and grace to raise them in a way that honors you and glorifies your name.

We entrust our precious children into your hands, knowing that you are the ultimate protector and provider. May your presence be felt in their lives every day, guiding them toward a future filled with hope, faith, and purpose. In Jesus' name, we pray. Amen.

CHAPTER THIRTEEN

THE MISTAKE OF NEGLECTING THE HOLY SPIRIT

This may very well be the most crippling mistake that we can make as Christians after accepting Jesus Christ as our Lord and Savior. I say this because if we embrace the Holy Spirit, it will negate the other 12 mistakes that I mentioned, including ones I didn't address. I believe the Holy Spirit is misunderstood in many ways: who He is, who He is not, His purpose, and why we as Christians must recognize and embrace Him.

So... who is the Holy Spirit? The Holy Spirit is the third person of the Holy Trinity or Godhead. He is the spirit and power of God. I repeat, the Holy Spirit is the power source of God; He is the power. He's the Comforter, Advocate, and Helper of God. He is the giver and keeper of the 9 gifts of the spirit. The Holy Spirit is the one who determines who receives gifts of the spirit, not Jesus or God, but the Holy Spirit oversees this. (**1 Corinthians 12:11**): "All these are the work of one and the same Spirit, and he distributes them to each one, just as he determines."

The nine gifts of the Holy Spirit are:

1. Wisdom

2. Knowledge

3. Faith

4. Gifts of healing

5. Working of miracles

6. Prophecy

7. Gift to distinguish between spirits

8. Various kinds of tongues

9. Interpretation of tongues.

All of these gifts can be found in (**1 Corinthians 12:8-10**). These gifts are believed to be bestowed upon individuals by the Holy Spirit to help them live a Christian life, serve others, and do the will of God. Paul tells us that we wrestle not against flesh and blood but against the powers of darkness in high places. Therefore, we need help! We need the Holy Spirit truly. Not embracing Him is like going into battle with weapons that have no ammunition. As Christians, God wants us to have power and authority through Him. Many of us get beaten up daily because we neglect the Holy Spirit and are ignorant of spiritual warfare. Even some Churches speak out against the Holy Spirit, which baffles me, but then again, not really because I know who the author of lies is. Therefore, Christians, read and study your Bibles and let no man, woman, or demon lead you astray. Every one of us is responsible for our own souls (1 Corinthians 16:13-14).

Since time immemorial, religious scholars and believers alike have explored the mysteries surrounding the Holy Spirit in an attempt to grasp its importance, role, and relation to humanity. Christian beliefs describe God as their constant companion and guide, believing He offers comfort, wisdom, and transformative power. As we explore the Holy Spirit, we will delve into its biblical origins, unmask its varied roles, and uncover its profound impact on believers throughout history.

The Holy Spirit, also referred to as the Holy Ghost, is an essential figure in Christian theology and has long been studied by scholars. Many texts have explored this concept extensively by looking at its roots in biblical literature as well as exploring its implications on modern faith practices. This chapter intends to delve into its nature, roles, and symbols while exploring its place within modern churches today.

The Bible gives an in-depth account of the Holy Spirit in its New Testament passages, where His nature is deeply interwoven with those of God the Father and Jesus Christ the Son. According to most Christian churches' doctrine of the Holy Trinity, His role is co-equal and co-eternal with these divine figures; His nature being divine, He participates fully in God's being, actions, and attributes - something both early church fathers and later theologians emphasized when teaching about this three-in-one relationship.

Furthermore, the role of the Holy Spirit cannot be overestimated in Christian history. Many branches of Christianity view Him as God's power active in this world today, dealing with both believers and non-believers on an individual level. Scripture records His role in creation, Jesus' incarnation, earthly ministry, and the growth of the early Church, as reflected in the Book of Acts; today, that presence continues through the life-mission worship of Christianity worldwide.

Individual believers rely on the Holy Spirit as the source of spiritual life; He regenerates, sanctifies, and sustains their faith while bestowing gifts for service and spiritual transformation. Through Him, they find guidance, conviction, and comfort, always leading back to Jesus Christ and God's Word.

The Holy Spirit can also be symbolized through various biblical texts. A dove, representing peace, purity, and divine approval, is often associated with Jesus' baptism, while the wind represents His invisible but dynamic influence; fire symbolizes its cleansing, refining, and illuminating power.

Furthermore, the Holy Spirit plays a central role in shaping Church life. He guides believers to understand and apply biblical texts accurately, provides spiritual gifts to strengthen one another spiritually while reaching out to those outside our faith tradition, fosters unity among Christians as a living body under Jesus' headship, fosters love between Christians themselves - truly making our Church an organism under His direction!

Conclusion The Holy Spirit is at the core of Christian belief. A precious and potency presence, its roles in creation, redemption, and sanctification can be seen both through Scripture and individual experience. Through symbols it reveals divine truths as it keeps the Church alive by leading it, strengthening it, and binding it together in love - thus its understanding and appreciation are fundamental for Christian living and spiritual development.

Consider these Bible verses from the Old Testament establishing the presence and power of the Holy Spirit from the very beginning:

1. (Genesis 1:2) - "The earth was formless and empty, and darkness covered the deep waters. And the Spirit of God was hovering over the surface of the waters."

2. (Numbers 11:25) - "Then the Lord came down in the cloud and spoke to him. He took some of the Spirit that was on Moses and put it on the seventy leaders. When the Spirit rested on them, they prophesied, but they never did so again."

3. (1 Samuel 10:6) - "The Spirit of the Lord will come powerfully upon you, and you will prophesy with them, and you will be changed into a different person."

4. (Isaiah 61:1) - "The Spirit of the Sovereign Lord is on me, because the Lord has anointed me to proclaim good news to the poor. He has sent me to bind up the brokenhearted, to proclaim freedom for the captives and release from darkness for the prisoners."

5. (Ezekiel 36:27) - "And I will put my Spirit in you and move you to follow my decrees and be careful to keep my laws."

These verses from the Old Testament show the Holy Spirit at work, either in creation, empowering individuals for specific tasks, or guiding and transforming individuals for God's purposes.

Now, consider these verses from the New Testament regarding the Holy Spirit:

1. (John 14:26) - "But the Advocate, the Holy Spirit, whom the Father will send in my name, will teach you all things and remind you of everything I have said to you."

2. (John 16:13) - "But when he, the Spirit of truth, comes, he will guide you into all the truth. He will not speak on his own; he will speak only what he hears, and he will tell you what is yet to come."

3. (Acts 1:8) - "But you will receive power when the Holy Spirit comes on you; and you will be my witnesses in Jerusalem, and in all Judea and Samaria, and to the ends of the earth."

4. (Acts 2:38) - "Peter replied, 'Repent and be baptized, every one of you, in the name of Jesus Christ for the forgiveness of your sins. And you will receive the gift of the Holy Spirit.'"

5. (Romans 8:26) - "In the same way, the Spirit helps us in our weakness. We do not know what we ought to pray for, but the Spirit himself intercedes for us through wordless groans."

6. (Galatians 5:22-23) - "But the fruit of the Spirit is love, joy, peace, forbearance, kindness, goodness, faithfulness, gentleness and self-control. Against such things, there is no law."

7. (Romans 14:17) - "For the kingdom of God is not a matter of eating and drinking but of righteousness and peace and joy in the Holy Spirit."

These verses highlight the role of the Holy Spirit as a teacher, guide, and source of power for believers. Overall, Jesus teaches that the Holy Spirit will be a constant presence in the lives of believers, guiding them in truth and empowering them to live out their faith in the world.

PRAYER OF SALVATION

I f you are an unbeliever who acquired this book and you feel the power of God moving on your heart, and you want to accept Jesus Christ as your Lord and Savior, I've included a prayer for you below:

Let's pray together. In the name of Jesus, I acknowledge that you died for my sins and rose from the dead on the third day. I understand that you are the only path to God. I accept you as my Lord and Savior. I invite you to come into my heart, my life, and my soul. I also ask you, Father God, to forgive me for my sins and my disbelief. In the name of Jesus, Amen.

You're now saved! Welcome to the body of Christ! All of the Host in Heaven celebrates you joyfully (Luke 15:7). I pray that the Lord leads you to a Church where you can learn and continue your walk with Christ. Above all, secure a Bible and begin studying God's Word.

ABOUT THE
AUTHOR

Travis Peagler is a devoted Christian, a committed husband, and a caring father. His dedication to writing has earned him accolades as an award-winning author.

With a commitment to faith and spirituality, Travis ensures that his writings reflect his beliefs and values. He is known for infusing his work with a "God Stamp", symbolizing his dedication to signing all of his creations in Jesus's name.

Through his diverse and impactful writings, Travis aims to inspire and uplift readers, spreading positivity and the message of faith. His work transcends genres and resonates with audiences of all backgrounds.

Join Travis Peagler on his literary journey, where words are infused with the divine and stories are a testament to the power of faith.

www.TravisPeagler.com

ACKNOWLEDGMENTS

First, I want to express my gratitude to God. I understand that this is not an awards ceremony or a speech of acceptance, but I am truly thankful to God with all of my heart for making me a creative individual. Although there were times in my life when this talent felt like a burden, I now embrace it wholeheartedly. I am grateful for the gift of creativity, even when I struggled to find a place for it in my life. Being a creative person is challenging, but I appreciate God for giving me the ability to create and shape my own narrative in accordance with His plan. God has been my father, provider, therapist, minister, and guardian. Hey God, it's me, the little 'Clack Kid' from the Platts, and I thank you for making me a strong and beautiful person, both inside and out. I thank you for all that you have done and all that you will continue to do in my life.

In the name of Jesus, forever and always!

www.ingramcontent.com/pod-product-compliance
Lightning Source LLC
Chambersburg PA
CBHW071013120626
46546CB00003B/1073